GROWING UP

Susan Meredith

Designed by Roger Priddy

Illustrated by Sue Stitt,
Kuo Kang Chen and Rob McCaig

Edited by Robyn Gee and Cheryl Evans

Special consultants: Judy Cunnington
of the Marriage Guidance Council
and Fran Reader, Senior Registrar in
Obstetrics and Gynaecology at
University College Hospital, London.

Contents

AIDS information approved
by the Terrence Higgins Trust

First published in 1985 by
Usborne Publishing Ltd
Usborne House, 83-85
Saffron Hill, London EC1N 8RT

The name Usborne and the
device ⬤ are Trade Marks of
Usborne Publishing Ltd. All
rights reserved.

Printed in Spain

© 1991, 1985 Usborne Publishing

About this book

You have been growing up since the day you were born. Just as a baby grows and changes as it becomes a child, so there is another, equally important, period of growth as you stop being a child and become an adult. This period is called adolescence, from the Latin word *adolescere*, meaning to grow up.

Adolescence

Adolescence lasts for several years, from the age of about 11 or younger up to the age of 18 or older. It involves all sorts of changes, both to your mind and emotions (psychological changes) and to your body (physical changes). This book concentrates mainly on explaining the physical changes.

Growing

On the first few pages you will find out about growth at adolescence and what changes you can expect in your voice and body shape.

Puberty

The physical changes of adolescence are called puberty from the Latin word *pubertas* which means adulthood. Most of them take place in the early years of adolescence.

Pages 8-9 will give you a general idea of the changes of puberty, how they happen and when. Then, on the following pages, they are all explained in more detail.

Sex and babies

The most important change of all is that you start being able to produce children, so there are sections on reproduction, sex and how contraception is used to prevent unwanted pregnancies on pages 16-33.

Your emotions

Although this book deals mainly with the physical changes of adolescence, your emotions are very important, too. Some of the confusing feelings you may experience are discussed on page 43.

Finding out more

There is further information about things that affect your body, such as food and drugs on pages 34-42. Then, on page 44, there is information about AIDS.

On pages 45-47 there is a glossary of difficult and technical terms. It includes definitions of some terms that do not appear in this book but which you may come across elsewhere. At the end of the book there are addresses and telephone numbers which may be helpful.

Growing

One of the earliest changes of puberty is that you suddenly grow taller very fast. This "growth spurt" is triggered by substances called hormones which are produced by special glands in your body. You will find out more about hormones and glands later on in the book.

During your growth spurt you grow as fast as you did when you were two years old. When a boy is growing at his fastest, he usually adds 7-12cm (2¾-4¾in) to his height in a single year. Girls add 6-11cm (2¼-4¼in).

On this page you can find out about how you grow and when you are likely to stop.

Height at age 10...

136cm (4ft 6in) 78%

138cm (4ft 6in) 84.4%

The pictures above show the average height of males and females at different ages and the percentage of their adult height that has been reached.

Girls start their growth spurt at about 10½ and boys at about 12½ so, for a while, girls tend to be taller than boys. Boys catch up by the time they are 14, though, and they still have some growing to do while girls have almost finished.

How tall will you be?

You can use the information in the chart on the right to estimate your eventual height. It tells you the percentage of your final height you are likely to have reached at any age during puberty. Here is the calculation you must do:

$$\frac{\text{Present height (in or cm)}}{\text{\% of full height (see chart)}} \times \frac{100}{1}$$

Here is an example, using centimetres, for a boy aged nine who is 130cm tall:

$$\frac{130}{75} \times \frac{100}{1} = \frac{520}{3} = 173.3$$

This boy is likely to be 173.3cm tall when he has finished growing.

Age	Per cent	
	Boys	Girls
8	72%	77.5%
9	75%	80.7%
10	78%	84.4%
11	81.1%	88.4%
12	84.2%	92.9%
13	87.3%	96.5%
14	91.5%	98.3%
15	96.1%	99.1%
16	98.3%	99.6%
17	99.3%	100%
18	99.8%	100%
19	100%	100%

at age 13 . . .

153cm
(5ft 0in)
87.3%

157cm
(5ft 2in)
96.5%

at age 19 . . .

175cm
(5ft 9in)
100%

163cm
(5ft 4in)
100%

Remember, all the ages and figures given in this book are averages only. Growth in height, like every other change of puberty, varies with the individual. The age at which you start your growth spurt bears no relation to your final height. This is determined mainly by what you have inherited from your parents. A few people do not go through a proper growth spurt at all but just get taller gradually instead.

How bones grow

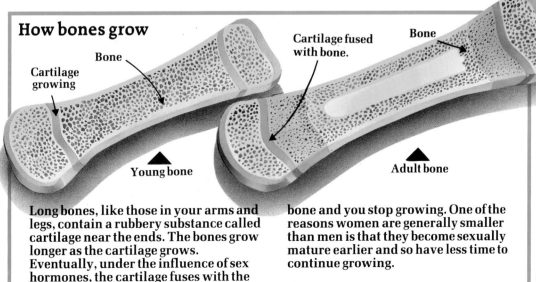

Bone

Cartilage
growing

Cartilage fused
with bone.

Bone

▲ **Young bone**

▲ **Adult bone**

Long bones, like those in your arms and legs, contain a rubbery substance called cartilage near the ends. The bones grow longer as the cartilage grows. Eventually, under the influence of sex hormones, the cartilage fuses with the bone and you stop growing. One of the reasons women are generally smaller than men is that they become sexually mature earlier and so have less time to continue growing.

5

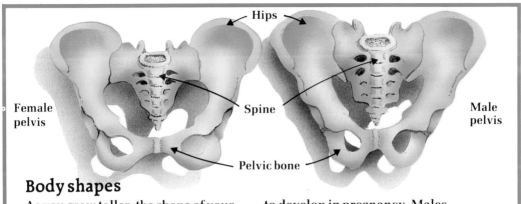

Female pelvis

Hips

Spine

Male pelvis

Pelvic bone

Body shapes

As you grow taller, the shape of your body changes too. Females develop broader hips as their pelvic bones widen. This gives more room for a baby to develop in pregnancy. Males generally develop broader shoulders, giving them added strength.

Voice changes

As the rest of your body grows, your voice box (larynx) also gets bigger and this makes your voice deeper. Most people's voices change very gradually but a few alter all at once. Males' voices go deeper than females' because males develop larger voice boxes. You can see this from the way the Adam's apple sticks out. Boys are sometimes embarrassed during puberty by their voices suddenly breaking into a squeak. This happens when the muscles of the larynx get out of control momentarily.

Enlarged picture of the voice box or larynx.

Adam's apple

Adam's apple

Vocal cords

Muscles

Face changes

You will notice that your face alters quite a lot at puberty. Some people describe it as coming down from under the skull. Your nose and jaw both become more prominent and your hairline recedes. Boys' faces alter more than girls'.

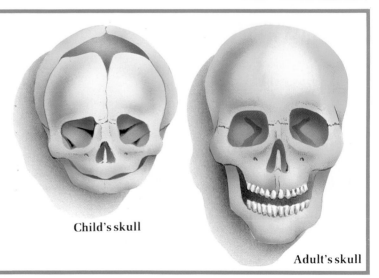

Child's skull

Adult's skull

Muscles

◀ As you grow up, your muscles increase in size and you get stronger. At birth, about 20% of your body is muscle. This increases to about 25% in early puberty and about 40% when you are adult. Men tend to have more muscle than women relative to their size. It is not true that you can "outgrow your strength" and so become weak and exhausted. Strength does lag behind muscle size though, so you may look stronger than you really are for a while.

Why are men stronger than women?

◀ In general men are stronger and have more stamina than women. This is not only because of their size, shape and muscles but also because they develop larger hearts and lungs than women relative to their size. The differences are often exaggerated by upbringing, when boys are encouraged to do more sports, for example, than girls. None of this makes men healthier than women and in fact women usually live longer.

The "ideal" figure

◀ Some people worry that they are not a certain shape or size. This is partly due to the "ideal" figures, especially of women, shown in advertisements, on TV, in films, in newspapers and magazines. In reality, different people find different body types attractive and, provided you are not very over or under weight, you do not need to worry.

Feeling gangly

▲ During your growth spurt your body does not all grow at the same rate. First, your feet and hands get bigger, then your arms and legs lengthen and, about a year later, the rest of your body grows. This may not be noticeable but some people are conscious of having oversized hands and feet for a while. It is not true that your co-ordination gets worse at puberty.

7

What happens at puberty?

When you reach puberty, all sorts of different changes start taking place in your body. The main purpose of them all is to enable you to start producing children. The main change is that your sex organs* grow and develop and start producing the special sex cells** from which babies can be made. You are not really aware of some of the changes going on, because they take place right inside your body. Others are much more obvious. The pictures on the right show some of the main changes of puberty.

Height increases suddenly.

Face alters.

Moustache and beard start to grow.

Voice gets deeper.

Shoulders and chest get broader.

Hair starts to grow under arms.

Pubic hair starts to grow.

Penis and testes get bigger. Male sex cells, called sperm, start being produced in the testes.

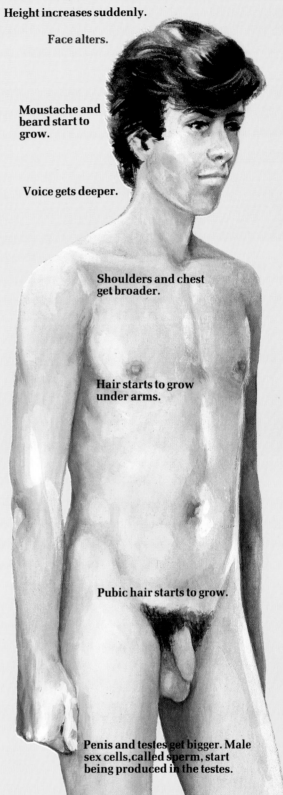

Secondary sexual features

Some of the changes that happen at puberty, such as beard growth and breast development, are not essential for producing children. Unlike the sex organs, which are known as primary sexual features, these are known as secondary sexual features. They are attractive to the opposite sex, acting as a signal that you are different from them.

*An organ is any part of your body which has a particular job to do.

Height increases suddenly.

Face alters.

Breasts develop.

Hair starts to grow
under arms.

Hips widen.

The circle of bone formed
by the hips is known as the
pelvis. There is a picture
of the pelvic bones on page 6.

Pubic hair starts to grow.

The ovaries, which are inside a female's
abdomen, enlarge and develop. Female
sex cells, called ova*** or egg cells,
develop in the ovaries. Periods start (see
pages 20-23).

**A cell is the smallest individual living
unit in the human body.

When does puberty start?

The age at which people
reach puberty varies
between the sexes and
also between individuals.
The average age is usually
said to be 11 for girls and
13 for boys. This is
misleading, though,
because girls can reach
puberty any time between
the ages of eight and 17
and boys any time
between 10 and 18.

This large timespan
means that two people
of the same age can be
very different. One of
them may have finished
developing physically
before the other has
even started.

This sometimes causes
embarrassment. It may
help to realize that
neither "early" nor
"late" development is
in any way abnormal.
Nor is one "better" than
the other.

The age at which you
reach puberty doesn't
affect what you will be
like as an adult.
Whether your body
matures slowly or
quickly, it will
continue until you are
fully-developed.

What determines the age
you reach puberty is
mainly the
characteristics you have
inherited from your
parents. Your build may
also play a part. Short,
stocky people tend to
develop earlier than tall,
thin people.

***The singular of ova is ovum.

9

How puberty starts

The changes that take place in your body during puberty all start in your brain and are caused by chemical substances called hormones. During childhood you have only low levels of certain hormones in your body and no-one knows quite what they do. At puberty your brain increases the levels of these hormones and this makes your body start producing the sex cells: ova and sperm. The level of other hormones, known as the sex hormones, also increases to bring about the rest of the changes of puberty.

Your brain and puberty

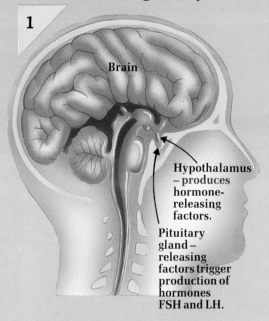

1

Brain

Hypothalamus – produces hormone-releasing factors.

Pituitary gland – releasing factors trigger production of hormones FSH and LH.

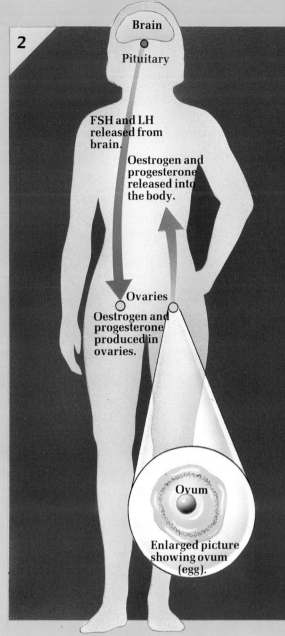

2

Brain

Pituitary

FSH and LH released from brain.

Oestrogen and progesterone released into the body.

Ovaries

Oestrogen and progesterone produced in ovaries.

Ovum

Enlarged picture showing ovum (egg).

Female ▲

Puberty starts in a tiny part of your brain called the hypothalamus. When this is sufficiently developed, it starts sending high levels of hormones to another part of your brain called the pituitary gland. The hormones from the hypothalamus are known as "releasing factors" because they trigger the pituitary to start releasing higher levels of two other hormones known as FSH and LH. *

The hormones FSH and LH make ova develop in girls' ovaries and start sperm production in boys' testes.

The ovaries and testes now start producing high levels of hormones of their own. These are the sex hormones. They help the ovaries and testes themselves to continue maturing and they also bring about other, more obvious changes of puberty, such as the

*The full names are Follicle Stimulating Hormone and Luteinizing Hormone.

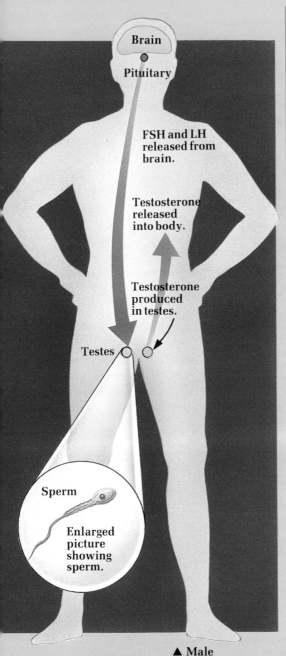

Brain

Pituitary

FSH and LH
released from
brain.

Testosterone
released
into body.

Testosterone
produced
in testes.

Testes

Sperm

Enlarged
picture
showing
sperm.

▲ Male

What are hormones?

1

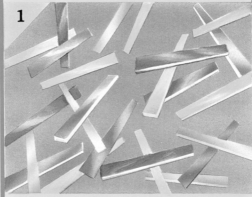

This picture shows crystals of the male
sex hormone, testosterone, magnified
thousands of times.* Many of the
changes that take place in males' bodies
at puberty are caused by testosterone.
There are many other types of
hormones in the human body besides
the ones to do with reproduction.
Adrenalin, for example, is a hormone
which prepares your body to take
emergency action when you are afraid
or angry.

2

Endocrine gland
▼

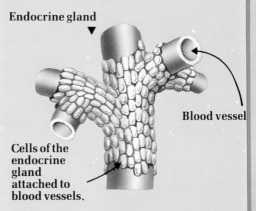

Blood vessel

Cells of the
endocrine
gland
attached to
blood vessels.

development of breasts in girls and the
growth of beards in boys. The most
important female sex hormones are
oestrogen and progesterone. The most
important male sex hormone is
testosterone.

The ovaries do not produce only
female sex hormones but also a low
level of male ones. In the same way, the
testes produce low levels of female sex
hormones in addition to male ones.

Hormones are produced in your body
in groups of cells called endocrine
glands. The pituitary, for example, is an
endocrine gland. The glands are
attached to blood vessels which have
thin walls. The hormones pass from the
glands through the walls and into your
blood. Your blood then carries them all
round your body. Different hormones
act on different parts of your body.

*In your body, hormones are in solution and look a greyish colour.

Hair

You grow hair on various parts of your body at puberty. Human beings are related to apes and the hair dates from a time when people were covered all over with quite thick hair. Hair growth at puberty is triggered by the sex hormones. The amount of hair you get depends on what you have inherited from your parents. *

Underarm hair

You usually start to get hair under your arms a year or two after your pubic hair begins to grow. No-one really knows what purpose the hair has.

In some countries many women remove the hair, though there is no medical reason for this. You will not sweat any less and the hair soon grows back again. If you do want to remove it, you can use a razor or special hair-removing cream. Be sure to follow the instructions with the cream carefully, as the skin under your arms is very sensitive.

Pubic hair

Female pubic hair

Male pubic hair

This is the hair which grows in the area of your external sex organs or "genitals" at puberty. It may help to cushion the pubic bone beneath it and is also a "secondary sexual feature". Although it is not essential for reproduction, it is generally attractive to the opposite sex.

At first, pubic hair is quite soft but it eventually becomes coarser than the hair on your head and curly. It is quite common for pubic hair to be a different colour from the hair on your head.

Hair on your body

Both males and females get hair on their arms and legs at puberty. Males in particular often get it on their chests too and sometimes on their abdomen, shoulders, back, hands and feet. Body hair shows up more on men than women because it is coarser. If your hair is dark, it will show up more than if it is fair.

Having a lot of hair does not make a man more "manly" or a woman in any way "unwomanly" and it has nothing to do with sexual ability. Although the hair is natural and normal, some women like to shave or use cream to remove it, especially from their legs. It is worth bearing in mind that the hair will grow back again, probably thicker and coarser than it was before.

*You can find out about the hair on your head on page 42.

Beards

The growth of a beard and moustache is usually one of the latest changes to happen to boys at puberty. First, hair grows on your upper lip, then on your cheeks and lastly on your chin. A lot of men have small hairless patches at the sides of their chin. At first, the hair is soft but it gradually gets coarser. It is not necessarily the same colour as the hair on your head. Some experts think that men's beards are the equivalent of roosters' combs and are an important secondary sexual feature.

Shaving

Some boys feel rather embarrassed when their beard begins to grow but you don't have to wait for a thick growth before you start shaving. On the other hand, you don't have to shave. If you decide to let your beard grow, make sure you keep it clean.

The quickest, most convenient way to shave is with an electric razor but many men find they get a closer shave using foam and warm water and a non-electric razor. It is easier to cut yourself this way though. Most men tend to shave in

Start at one ear and work round to chin. Shave downwards in direction of hairs or it may hurt.

Do other side of face, top lip and then under chin. For a closer shave, you can then try shaving upwards.

the way shown here.

If you find shaving makes your skin slightly sore, try dabbing on talcum powder afterwards.

Shaving in warm water opens up the pores of your skin. Splashing on cold water afterwards helps to close them up again. Aftershave lotion contains astringents, which do the same thing. They also sting when you first put the lotion on. Too much aftershave can make your skin dry and flaky.

It is unhygienic to use anyone else's razor (see also page 44).

Girls and facial hair

Many girls also get a fine covering of hair on their faces. It is not usually noticeable. If the hair is dark and you are unhappy about it, you can use cream to remove it or ask a beauty expert about dyeing it. Don't try to shave, as the skin is more sensitive than in males.

Stray hairs

You can find stray hairs growing anywhere on your body. Some people like to pluck them out or cut them off, especially if they are on their face. Don't pluck a hair which is growing out of a mole. Cut the hair instead.

Breasts

Developing breasts is one of the main changes of puberty for girls. The hormone oestrogen, produced by the ovaries, makes the breasts develop, starting usually at about age 11. Your nipples are the first things to grow.

As your breasts develop and enlarge, they may feel uncomfortable at times. Also, one breast may develop faster than the other. They will even out later, though no-one's breasts match exactly.

The age your breasts start developing has no bearing on their eventual size. Full breast size is usually reached at about age 17.

What are breasts made of?

The breast in this picture is drawn so that you can see what it is made of and how it works.

1

When a woman has a baby, a hormone from her pituitary gland triggers milk production in these parts of her breasts. The milk is made from substances which pass out of the woman's blood as it travels through her breasts.

2

Each breast contains between 15 and 20 of these tubes or "ducts". In childhood the ducts are very small but at puberty they enlarge and branch out. When milk is produced in the breasts after a woman has had a baby, it drains into these ducts and is stored there until the baby needs it.

3

The nipple is the most sensitive part of the breast. When it is stimulated by sensations such as touch or cold, tiny muscles around its base make it erect.

The shape of nipples varies. It is not unusual for the nipples to be turned inwards instead of outwards.

When a baby sucks at its mother's breast, a hormone from her pituitary allows the milk to flow out of the ducts through microscopic holes in the nipple.

What are breasts for?

The main purpose of breasts is to produce milk for feeding any babies a woman might have. They are also an important secondary sexual feature. They are attractive to men and are sensitive to touch, which increases the woman's sexual pleasure.

4

The area around the nipple is called the areola. Its colour varies from pink to dark brown, becoming darker as you get older and during pregnancy.

The tiny lumps in the areola are glands. During breast-feeding, these produce a fatty substance which helps to protect the nipples.

Stray hairs often grow in the areola. You can pluck these out or cut them off if you want to.

Breast size

A lot of women worry that their breasts are too big or too small. Like worries about general body shape, this may be due to images of "ideal" women given in the media. In reality, as it is fat and not the milk-producing or storing areas which determines the size of your breasts, all sizes are equally able to feed babies. They are also equally sensitive and men differ as to the size and shape they find most attractive.

5

As the milk-collecting ducts enlarge at puberty, fat is formed to provide a protective cushion for them. It is the amount of fat in your breasts which determines their size.

Boys and breasts

Some boys as well as girls seem to start developing breasts at puberty. This is nothing to worry about. You are not changing sex and the "breasts" will disappear within about 18 months as hormone production settles down.

6

The ducts are separated from each other by elastic fibres. These tend to stretch as you get older, which makes the breasts droop.

Bras

Whether or not you wear a bra is up to you. If you are comfortable without one, there is no medical reason for wearing one. The way the elastic fibres stretch and your breasts droop as you get older is quite natural and wearing a bra will not stop it happening. The weight of large breasts can sometimes tear the fibres or stretch them prematurely though, so if you have large breasts it may be a good idea to wear a bra most of the time. Most women find it more comfortable to wear a bra for doing exercises or sports.

Buying a bra

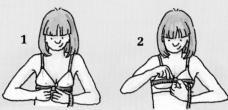

When you buy a bra you need to give your chest measurement and cup size.

1. To find out your chest size, measure just under your breasts around your ribcage and add 12cm (5in).
   e.g. 68cm (27in) + 12cm (5in) = size 80cm (32in).

2. To find out your cup size measure again around the fullest part of your breasts. If this is the same as the measurement above, you are an A cup; if there is a 2.5cm (1in) difference you are a B cup; a 5cm (2in) difference means you are a C cup.

Do exercises work?

No amount of exercising can increase your breast size because exercise works by building up muscle and there are no muscles in breasts.
   Exercise involving the chest muscles, such as swimming, will strengthen these muscles and may help them to support your breasts more easily.

Female sex organs

The growth and development of the sex organs is really the major change of puberty. It is what eventually enables you to have children. Girls are often unaware of the changes in their sex organs because most of them are inside their body.
   The picture on the opposite page shows the female sex organs which are outside the body. You can find out about the female sex organs inside the body on pages 18-19 and about the male sex organs on pages 24-25.
   External sex organs are called genitals. Girls' genitals are less obvious than boys'.

Vulva: the female genitals are called the vulva, which is the Latin word for opening. Here you can see the different parts. The only way you can really see your vulva is to use a mirror. Don't worry if yours looks different from the one in this picture. Genitals vary from person to person just like any other part of the body.

1
Outer labia: these are two thick folds of skin or "lips". They are made of fat and have pubic hair growing on them. They are normally closed over the inner parts of the vulva, protecting them.

2
Urinary opening: this is the opening of the "urethra", which is the tube leading from your bladder to the outside of your body. It is where your urine comes out.

3

Mons: this is a mound of fat which cushions and protects the pubic bone beneath it. Your pubic hair grows over it.

5

Clitoris: this is the most sensitive part of the female body. It is the equivalent of the male's penis, although it is only about the size of a pea. The exact size varies from woman to woman and is not related to sensitivity. Only the tip of the clitoris is visible. This has a fold of skin or "hood" over it, formed by the inner labia meeting at the front of the vulva.

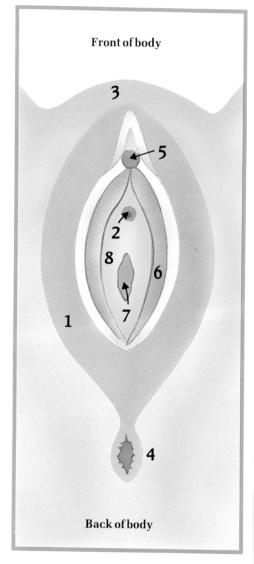

Front of body

Back of body

6

Inner labia: these are thinner than the outer labia and have no hair on them. As you grow up, they become increasingly sensitive to touch. A lubricating fluid is produced by glands in the labia. The left and right labia are rarely the same size. Sometimes the inner labia stick out from between the outer labia.

7

Vaginal opening: this is the opening to the vagina, which is a tube leading to your internal sex organs. It is where the blood comes out when you have a period (see page 20), where the penis fits during sex (see page 27) and where babies leave the body when they are born. Although the opening is very small, it stretches painlessly.

8

Hymen: This is a thin layer of skin which partially covers the vaginal opening. As your vagina grows and stretches during puberty, the hymen gradually breaks down. It is often broken before puberty, especially if you do a lot of sport. Even if your hymen still seems intact there will be enough tiny holes in it for period blood to get out.

4

Anus: this is the hole at the end of your digestive tract where the waste leaves your body when you go to the toilet.

Female sex organs inside the body

The picture on the right shows the internal female sex organs seen from the front. Most of them are drawn so that you can see inside. Like the rest of the body, the internal sex organs grow considerably at puberty. The weight of the uterus (womb) may increase by as much as 44g (1.62oz), for example.

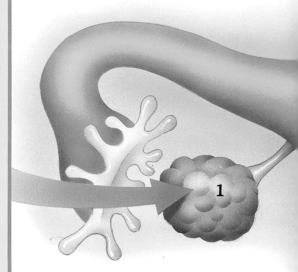

1

Ovaries: a female has two ovaries. They are low down in her abdomen, one on each side, and are attached to the outside of the uterus by connecting fibres. Fully developed ovaries are about the shape and size of shelled walnuts.

When a girl is born, she already has hundreds of thousands of ova (egg cells) stored in her ovaries. At puberty, the hormones FSH and LH produced by the pituitary make the ova begin to mature and be released from the ovaries. Usually one ovum is released each month, from alternate ovaries. This is called ovulation. The process continues until the age of about 50. The time when it stops is called the menopause.

Where are the internal sex organs?

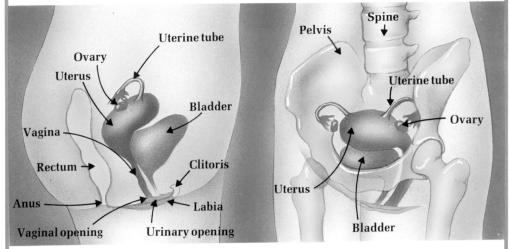

The two pictures above show the position of the female sex organs in the abdomen. The one on the left is a sideways view, so you can see where the organs are in relation to the bladder and rectum (back passage) and how they connect up with the external sex organs described on the previous page. The picture on the right shows how the organs (especially the uterus) are protected by the bones of the pelvis.

2

Uterine tubes: the uterine, or Fallopian, tubes, are muscular tubes. They are about 12cm (4¾in) long and the thickness of a pencil. The hollow part is only the width of the lead of a pencil.

When an ovum is released from an ovary, the fringed end of the nearest uterine tube swoops down and draws it into the tube. The muscular walls of the tube and tiny hairs inside it then move the ovum along towards the uterus.

It is while an ovum is in the uterine tube that a woman may become pregnant if she has sex. A sperm cell (from the man's body) may "fertilize" the ovum. You can find out how this happens on page 30.

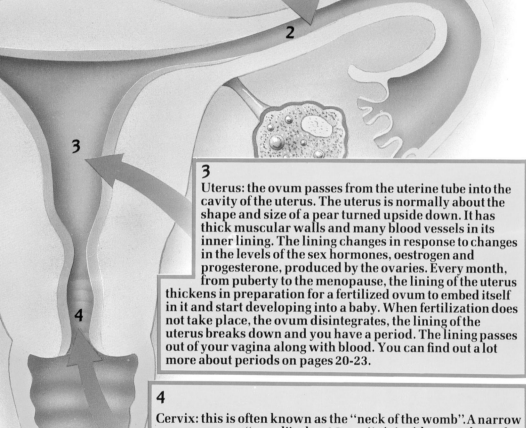

3

Uterus: the ovum passes from the uterine tube into the cavity of the uterus. The uterus is normally about the shape and size of a pear turned upside down. It has thick muscular walls and many blood vessels in its inner lining. The lining changes in response to changes in the levels of the sex hormones, oestrogen and progesterone, produced by the ovaries. Every month, from puberty to the menopause, the lining of the uterus thickens in preparation for a fertilized ovum to embed itself in it and start developing into a baby. When fertilization does not take place, the ovum disintegrates, the lining of the uterus breaks down and you have a period. The lining passes out of your vagina along with blood. You can find out a lot more about periods on pages 20-23.

4

Cervix: this is often known as the "neck of the womb". A narrow passageway or "canal", about 2mm (⅛in) wide, runs through the cervix, connecting the uterus and vagina. When a woman gives birth the canal gets much wider to let the baby pass through.

5

Vagina: this is a muscular tube, about 10cm (4in) long, connecting the uterus with the outside of the body. Normally the walls of the vagina are quite close together but they are arranged in folds rather like a concertina. This means they can stretch enormously and painlessly, enough to let a baby be born. Glands in the lining of the vagina produce a cleansing and lubricating fluid.

Periods

Starting to have periods is probably the single most important change of puberty for girls. On these two pages you can see how periods come about because the lining of the uterus breaks down and causes a small amount of bleeding from the vagina. This may sound rather frightening but, if you are prepared for it, it is nothing at all to worry about. The blood trickles out gradually over a few days and good-quality tampons or sanitary towels (STs) can easily cope with the flow.

Periods can start any time between the age of nine and 18 but the most usual time is about a year after your breasts have begun to develop.

What is a period?

Many people first notice a period has started when they go to the toilet.

You appear to lose only blood when you have a period but the flow really consists of cells from the lining of the uterus which are simply stained by blood and mixed with a sticky fluid from the cervix. The blood comes from small blood vessels in the uterus which tear as the lining comes away from the walls. On average you lose about two tablespoons of blood per period. A period can last from two to about eight days but the average is four.

Hormones and periods

Here you can see how the menstrual cycle is controlled by hormones. The cycle given here is an average one lasting 28 days. Yours may be different.

Day 1

The period starts. At the same time, the hormone FSH from the pituitary is making an ovum mature in a tiny sac or "follicle" in one of the ovaries.

Day 5

The ovum continues to mature and the follicle starts to move towards the surface of the ovary. The follicle is producing the hormone oestrogen. This makes the lining of the uterus start to thicken again. At the moment it is probably about 1mm (1/16 in) thick and the period is over.

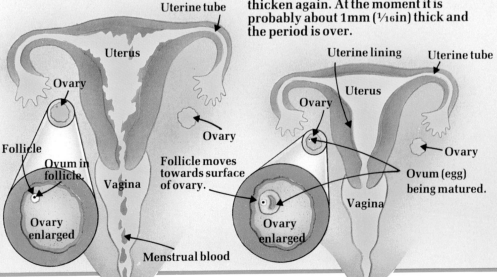

Uterine tube

Uterus

Ovary

Follicle

Ovum in follicle.

Vagina

Ovary

Ovary enlarged

Follicle moves towards surface of ovary.

Menstrual blood

Uterine lining

Uterine tube

Uterus

Ovary

Ovary

Ovum (egg) being matured.

Vagina

Ovary enlarged

How often do periods happen?

Another name for periods is menstruation. This comes from the Latin word *mensis* which means month. On average, a woman has a period about every four weeks (28 days). The cycle can vary though from about 20 days to 35 from woman to woman and even in the same woman from month to month.

Myths about periods

Over the centuries there have been many myths about periods. Most date from the time when the cause of them was not understood. Odd superstitions survive even today, such as you should not wash your hair when you have a period or eat ice cream. In reality, a woman can do everything she normally does, including having a bath or shower, and swimming.

Day 14

The pituitary stops producing FSH and produces LH instead. This makes the now mature ovum burst out of its follicle and leave the ovary (ovulation). The empty follicle, known as the "yellow body", starts to produce the second female sex hormone, progesterone, as well as oestrogen. Progesterone makes the thickening lining of the uterus soft and spongy so that if the ovum is fertilized it can embed itself.

Day 21

The ovum has arrived in the uterus. If it has not been fertilized, both it and the yellow body start to disintegrate and the levels of oestrogen and progesterone fall. By this time, the lining of the uterus is about 5mm (¼in) thick. It starts to disintegrate and come away from the walls of the uterus. Some of the blood vessels kink and tear in the process. On day 1 the next period starts and the cycle begins again.

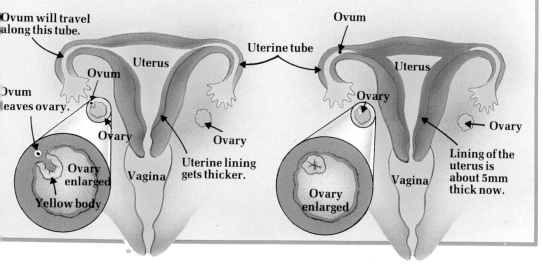

Ovum will travel along this tube.

Ovum leaves ovary.

Uterine tube

Uterus

Ovum

Ovary

Ovary enlarged

Yellow body

Ovary

Vagina

Uterine lining gets thicker.

Ovum

Uterus

Ovary

Ovary

Lining of the uterus is about 5mm thick now.

Vagina

Ovary enlarged

What to wear

You have a choice of using either sanitary towels or tampons to absorb menstrual blood. Towels soak up the blood as it leaves your body from the vaginal opening whereas tampons fit right inside the vagina and catch it before it leaves your body. Both towels and tampons are quite expensive. You may see free samples offered in magazine advertisements. It is worth sending off for these so you can decide which type and make you prefer.

Towels

These come in different sizes and thicknesses so you can choose one to match the heaviness of your period.

Peel-off paper

Looped towel

Sticky stripe

About 20cm (8in) long

"Press-on" towels have a sticky stripe on the back which you press to your pants to hold the towel in place. These are the most comfortable type of towel, though occasionally they can crease up or come slightly unstuck.

If you buy towels with loops, you will also need a special belt which you buy separately. This type of towel tends to be bulky.

Changing towels

It is best to change your towel every few hours even if your flow is not heavy. Menstrual blood is perfectly clean but once outside your body it meets bacteria from the air and this can cause a smell or even an infection. Look for towels which say "completely flushable" on the packet. Others will not flush down the toilet or may block it, so you have to wrap them up and put them in the dustbin. In public toilets you are usually asked to put all towels in one of the paper bags provided and throw them in the bin or incinerator.

Problems with periods

Menstruation is a normal, healthy process, not an illness, and many women have no problems at all with periods. On the other hand, the female hormone cycle is very complex. Whereas a male's sex hormone levels remain more or less the same from day to day, a female's are changing every day over the course of her cycle. The hormones are carried in your bloodstream, so they can affect other parts of your body besides your sex organs. This makes some people feel unwell or irritable before or during their period.

Painful periods

Quite a lot of women get an ache or cramp-like pains in their lower abdomen at the start of a period. Doctors think this is caused by hormones making the muscles of the uterus contract (get smaller). If the pain is only slight, exercise can help. If it is quite bad, you may need to take a painkiller and lie down with a hot water bottle. The medical name for period pain is dysmenorrhea.*

*Pronounced dis-men-or-ear.

Tampons

Many women prefer tampons to towels for various reasons. Once a tampon is in the right position in your vagina, you cannot feel it at all. You do not need to worry about people seeing the shape of a towel through close-fitting trousers. You can have a bath or go swimming. All tampons can be flushed down the toilet and they are easier to carry around because they are smaller and individually wrapped. You do not need to worry about any smell.

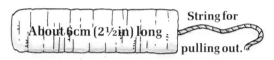

About 6cm (2½in) long

String for pulling out.

Changing tampons

It is not as easy to tell when a tampon needs changing as it is a towel, though you can sometimes feel a bubbling sensation just before the tampon starts to leak and the string may become bloodstained. You should change tampons at least every six hours anyway, and as soon as you wake up after a night's sleep. If you leave them in too long, bacteria in the vagina may cause an infection.

Inserting a tampon

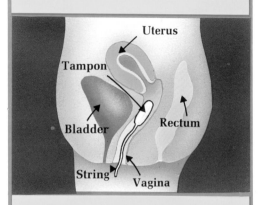

Some girls do not want to try tampons when they first start their periods but there is no reason not to if you feel like it. Start with the smallest size; you can always go on to larger ones if they cannot cope with your flow. Tampons come with instructions and you should follow these carefully. The best time to try inserting a tampon for the first time is when your flow is heaviest. Always wash your hands before unwrapping a tampon to guard against infection and if you drop one on the floor, don't use it. If you can't get a tampon in, it probably means that your hymen is still fairly intact. Try again in a few months, when it may have broken more.

Pre-menstrual tension (PMT)

Some women suffer from PMT for a few days before the start of a period. Like period pain, PMT is probably caused by hormones. Symptoms include sore, swollen breasts, a bloated, heavy feeling especially in the abdomen, headaches, spots, tiredness and feeling tense, bad-tempered or depressed. There is still no proven medical remedy but your doctor should be able to give you some tips.

Irregular periods

This is not necessarily a problem. It is quite usual for periods to be irregular for the first year or two. This is because your hormones have not yet got into a regular rhythm. You may even find that several months pass between periods. Other reasons for periods becoming irregular include being ill, feeling upset or worried about something and even going on holiday.

28 days is the average cycle, but yours may be longer or shorter.

Male sex organs

It is easy for a boy to tell when his sex organs are developing because they increase visibly in size. The testes start to get bigger and the penis follows about a year later. The picture on the right shows the male sex organs viewed from the front. They are drawn so that you can see the different parts.

1

Testes: the male's testes are the equivalent of the female's ovaries. They produce male sex cells (sperm) and the male sex hormone testosterone. The testes are about the size of small plums. The left testis* usually hangs lower than the right. From puberty on, sperm cells are formed continuously in tiny, coiled tubes inside the testes. It takes over two months for a sperm to be formed. Several million sperm complete the process every day. Unlike the ovaries, the testes do not stop producing sex cells during middle age. Production continues, though at a lower level, right into old age.

2

Scrotum: the testes are contained in a loose pouch of wrinkled skin called the scrotum. They are outside the abdomen as sperm are only produced at a temperature about 2°C lower than normal internal body temperature. When your testes are exposed to cold, the skin of your scrotum shrinks, drawing them closer to your body for warmth.

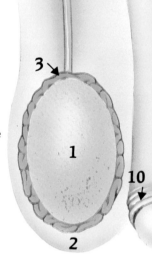

Position of the sex organs

This picture shows the male sex organs viewed from the right.

Bladder

Seminal vesicle

Rectum

Anus

Prostate gland

Sperm duct

Epididymis

Testis

Scrotum

Foreskin

Glans

Penis

Urethra

3

Epididymis: the epididymis is a coiled tube which lies over the back of each testis. Each tube would be 6m (20ft) long if it was uncoiled. The sperm cells are squeezed from the testes into the epididymis, where they mature for about two weeks.

4

Sperm ducts: these are two tubes, about 40cm (16in) long, which lead from the epididymis up into the pelvis. There they join into the urethra as it leaves the bladder. The tubes are muscular and about the thickness of string. The sperm travel along the tubes from the epididymis towards the penis.

*This is the singular of testes.

5

Seminal vesicles: these are glands. They produce a nourishing fluid which helps to give the sperm energy.

6

Prostate gland: this is about the size of a walnut and produces a fluid which helps the sperm to move.

7

Urethra: this is longer in males than females and has two functions. One is to carry urine to the outside of the body. During sexual excitement it carries semen, which is the mixture of sperm and the fluids produced by the seminal vesicles and prostate gland.

8

Penis: usually the penis is quite small and soft. During sexual excitement, more blood flows into it than usual, and less flows out, so it becomes larger and harder and stands away from the body (an erection). This enables it to fit inside the female's vagina. Sperm can be deposited in the vagina so that a baby can be made.

9

Glans: this is the name for the tip of the penis, which is the most sensitive part.

10

Foreskin: this is the fold of skin which covers the glans of the penis. Glands under the foreskin produce a white, creamy substance called smegma. This helps the skin slide back smoothly over the glans.

- 7

8

9

9

Circumcision

In some cultures, for example the Jewish one, it is customary to cut away a boy's foreskin surgically a few days after birth. This is called circumcision. Although the operation is usually performed for religious reasons, some people believe it is also more hygienic. When the foreskin is intact, smegma can accumulate beneath it, causing a smell or occasionally an infection. However, if you roll back your foreskin and wash gently underneath it every day, you will probably avoid this problem.

Penis size

The size of unerect penises varies from male to male and has no relation to body size. Some boys worry about having a small penis. In fact, small penises generally increase their size a lot more than large ones when they become erect, so that apparent differences become much less. The average length of an erect penis is between 12½ and 17½cm (5 and 6¾in). A smaller erect penis does not make any difference to either the male's or female's sexual pleasure.

Sex

As the level of your sex hormones increases and your sex organs mature, you gradually become more aware of sexual feelings. This may start with an increased awareness of your own body and emotions, which develops to include a new interest in the opposite sex. At first this often takes the form of dreams and fantasies. Later this becomes a desire for physical contact and ultimately for sexual intercourse.

In many countries sexual intercourse is illegal under a certain age (called the "age of consent" – 16 in Britain for example). This does not mean that, having reached the age of consent, you have to have sexual intercourse. You should not let anyone pressure you into it before you feel completely ready and have considered all the possible consequences, including unwanted pregnancy and disease, for example, AIDS (see pages 28, 30-33 and 44).

Touching, stroking and kissing

Most people have quite a lot of physical contact of a non-sexual kind with their family and close friends, which may involve touching and kissing. The line between sexual and non-sexual contact is not a clear one.

The areas of the body that are the most sexually sensitive are called the erogenous zones. These include the genitals, lips, breasts and buttocks, but ear-lobes, feet and many other areas are sensitive in different people.

"Snogging", "petting" and "necking" are all slang words used to describe sexual kissing, touching and stroking. The erogenous zones tend to be touched most.

Sexual contact often involves touching or stroking areas of another person's body that you would not normally touch in a non-sexual relationship, such as the breasts or genitals.

Deep kissing on the lips, sometimes called "French kissing", when one or both partners put their tongue in the other's mouth also frequently forms a part of sexual contact.

Sexual touching and kissing of this kind usually create a feeling of intense pleasure in both partners and may lead to a desire for sexual intercourse. You can find out about sexual intercourse on the page opposite.

Sexual intercourse

1. Strictly speaking, sexual intercourse begins when a male's penis enters a female's vagina, and ends when it is withdrawn. However, intercourse, or "making love", is almost always preceded by a period of touching, stroking and kissing known as "foreplay".

2. Once the penis is inside the vagina, one or both partners move their pelvis, so that it slides in and out repeatedly. This creates a sensation of pleasure.

This stage can last from a few minutes to over an hour, with changes of rhythm and rest periods.

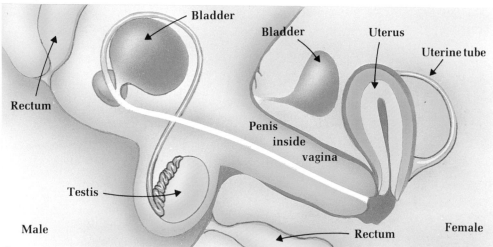

3. Eventually, because of the stimulation to the penis and the clitoris, orgasm usually occurs.

This is the climax of sexual excitement both for males and females. It is often called "coming". An orgasm consists of a series of brief muscular spasms (contractions) in the sex organs. These are felt as a throbbing or pulsating sensation, which spreads through the whole body, and cause a feeling of intense pleasure followed by a feeling of relaxation.

One partner may reach orgasm before the other, or a couple may have their orgasms at the same time. Orgasm may not occur every time, especially in females. In males semen is squirted (ejaculated) out of the penis by the muscular contractions.

Changes in the body

Sexual excitement brings about a whole range of changes in the body.

In women's bodies glands in the vagina produce a lubricating fluid, so that the penis can enter it more easily. The breasts may get larger and the nipples become erect.

In men's bodies the penis becomes larger and harder and points upwards at an angle away from the body (an erection), enabling it to fit into the vagina. The testes swell and are drawn closer to the body.

In both sexes muscles all over the body become tense, the heart beats faster, blood pressure rises and breathing becomes faster and shallower. The chest, (especially in females) and the face may become flushed.

Ejaculation

The semen that is ejaculated from the penis at orgasm is a mixture of sperm (male sex cells) and fluids produced by the prostate gland and the seminal vesicles (see page 25).

On average, only a small teaspoonful of semen comes out of the penis with each ejaculation, but this contains hundreds of millions of sperm.

The muscular contractions of orgasm squeeze the sperm from their storage place near the testes, through sperm ducts to the urethra, which leads from the bladder through the centre of the penis. Muscles around the base of the bladder act as a valve and ensure that urine cannot pass down the urethra at the same time as semen.

Sex and emotions

Sex is not just about physical sensations; it usually involves very strong emotions as well. How people feel about it usually depends a great deal on how emotionally involved they are with their partner and on how much they trust them.

Problems with sex often have emotional causes. Anxiety, shyness, fear and unhappiness can all have physical effects on the body.

One of the few occasions when a problem with sex is likely to be purely physical is if a woman experiences slight pain and bleeding when the penis pierces the hymen* the first time she has intercourse. (In many women, the hymen has been stretched or broken before this by doing sport or using tampons.)

Sex and pregnancy

Once a girl has started ovulating (releasing eggs) and having periods, there is always a chance that sexual intercourse could make her pregnant, unless special precautions are taken to prevent a baby from starting. These precautions are known as contraception (meaning "against conception"). On pages 30-33 you can find out about the contraceptive methods used to prevent pregnancy.

Homosexuality

Homosexuality means being sexually attracted only by people of your own sex. *Homo* comes from the Greek word meaning the same. (Heterosexuals are people who are sexually attracted to the opposite sex, *heteros* being the Greek word for other.)

It is quite normal to experience strong feelings for someone of the same sex, especially during puberty. This is different from true homosexuality, when people are attracted only to people of the same sex right into adulthood.

It is thought that about one in ten people are homosexual or "gay" Female homosexuality is often called lesbianism. Many more people are bi-sexual, which means they are attracted to both sexes.

The cause of homosexuality is not really understood. In some people it may be biological, in others it is more likely to be psychological.

Sexually transmitted diseases (STDs)

These are also known as venereal diseases (VD). They are infections in the sex organs caused by microbes (microscopic living creatures) which are passed from one person's body to another's during sexual contact.

There are many different types of STDs. Some affect both sexes; some affect only males and some only females. A few can develop without sexual contact.

The first symptoms of many of the diseases are similar. They can include itching or soreness of the genitals or anus; a discharge; a sore, lump or rash near the genitals or anus; pain when going to the toilet.

One of the problems with STDs is that people can sometimes have a disease and infect a partner without knowing it, because they have no symptoms.

Almost all STDs can be cured if they are treated early enough by a doctor. One very important exception to this is AIDS (see page 44).

28

The hymen is described on page 17.

Fantasies

It is quite common to fantasize during puberty, especially during masturbation. Some people fantasize about someone they know, or about famous people, such as pop stars. Others make up imaginary characters. You may be surprised or troubled at the form some of your fantasies take. This is quite normal. Fantasies give you the opportunity to imagine doing things that might be unacceptable if you were actually to do them.

Masturbation

Masturbation means handling the genitals to give sexual pleasure, either to yourself or to someone else.

Males generally masturbate by rubbing the penis rhythmically backwards and forwards in their hand, while females generally rub the area around the clitoris rhythmically with their fingers. This may eventually lead to an orgasm (see page 27).

There used to be many myths about the bad effects masturbation could have. In fact, masturbation only becomes unhealthy if someone wants to do it all the time.

Males tend to masturbate more than females during puberty. This may be partly because the penis is more accessible than the clitoris and males grow up used to touching it every time they go to the toilet.

Wet dreams

These are quite common in boys during puberty. While you are asleep you have an erection and ejaculate semen. This happens because your body has not quite got used to its new way of working. It happens during dreaming though not necessarily about sex.

If you are embarrassed about staining the sheets, you can sponge the stain out with soap and cold water, or keep paper tissues or a toilet roll near the bed for mopping up.

Embarrassing erections

Most males are embarrassed by having erections at inconvenient moments during puberty. Most erections are triggered by a sexual thought, for example, when you see a girl you like. Some happen when your genitals are accidentally stimulated, for example, by the vibrations of a moving train. The best way to make the erection subside is to concentrate very hard on something else.

It is quite common for males to wake up with an erection in the morning. This is due to dreaming, though not necessarily about sex.

Contraception

The moment when a woman becomes pregnant after having sexual intercourse is called conception or fertilization. There are various measures a couple can take to prevent pregnancy. This is called contraception (against conception). Some methods of contraception are much more effective than others. In many countries they are provided free through family doctors or at special clinics.

Conception

When a male ejaculates semen inside a female's vagina during intercourse, hundreds of millions of sperm cells are deposited close to the cervix. From there, sperm swim up through the uterus and into the uterine tubes. Only about 100 sperm get as far as the tubes before they die. If there is an ovum in one of the tubes, the sperm cluster around it and one sperm may join with it. This is conception or fertilization. Together the ovum and sperm make one new cell. This grows and develops into a baby in the female's uterus.

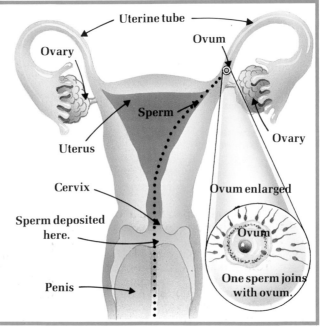

Uterine tube

Ovum

Ovary

Sperm

Ovary

Uterus

Cervix

Ovum enlarged

Sperm deposited here.

Ovum

Penis

One sperm joins with ovum.

Combined pill

This is the most effective method of contraception. The woman takes a pill a day for three weeks in every four. The pills contain a combination of oestrogen and progesterone. They work by lowering the output of the hormones FSH and LH from her pituitary so that no ova mature in her ovaries and ovulation cannot take place.

The pill has to be prescribed by a doctor and the woman has regular check-ups to make sure she is not suffering from any side effects. These can

Some women put on weight.

include weight gain, headaches, nausea, sore breasts and, in very rare cases, high blood pressure or even a thrombosis (blood clot), especially in the legs. A woman is not prescribed the pill in the first place if the doctor thinks she is especially likely to suffer serious side effects.

One good side effect of the pill is that periods become lighter, more regular and more pain-free. For this reason it is sometimes specially prescribed for women with period problems.

Packet of pills.

Mini-pill

This is slightly less effective than the combined pill and is taken every day. The pills contain progesterone only and work by altering the lining of the cervix so that sperm find it difficult to enter the uterus. They also ensure that if an ovum is fertilized it cannot embed itself. (The combined pill does these things too, as well as preventing ovulation.) The mini-pill is also prescribed by a doctor and the woman has regular check-ups. It has fewer known side effects than the combined pill but it is still quite new so its use has to be monitored. One side effect is that it tends to make periods irregular.

IUD (Intra-uterine device), or coil

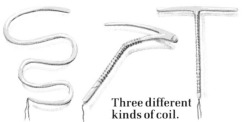

Three different kinds of coil.

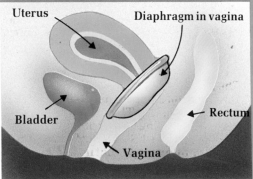

An IUD is a small coil or loop of plastic, like the ones shown above, which is inserted into the woman's uterus. It works partly by preventing a fertilized ovum from embedding itself in the lining of the uterus.

The coil is inserted by a doctor, through the woman's vagina, and can then be kept in place for a few years, without her being aware of it. The woman checks regularly that it has not fallen out by feeling for a thread which is left hanging down into her vagina. IUDs sometimes cause heavy or painful periods. They also increase the risk of infections, which can make the woman sterile (incapable of having children).

Diaphragm or cap

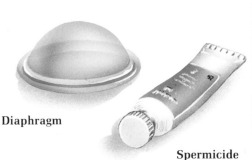

Diaphragm

Spermicide

A diaphragm is a thin, cap-shaped piece of rubber which fits over the cervix and helps to prevent sperm from entering the uterus. To be effective the diaphragm has to be smeared with a "spermicide". This is a cream or jelly containing special chemicals which help to kill sperm.*

The woman has to be measured for a diaphragm by a doctor. She then inserts the diaphragm herself before having intercourse and leaves it in for several hours afterwards, for the spermicide to act. Neither she nor the man can feel the diaphragm during intercourse.

*Spermicides are not effective used on their own.

Condom or sheath

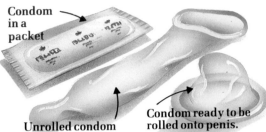

Condom in a packet

Unrolled condom

Condom ready to be rolled onto penis.

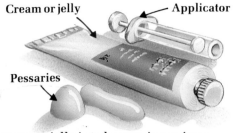

Cream or jelly

Applicator

Pessaries

A condom (johnny or rubber in slang) is a thin rubber sheath which is put on to the man's erect penis before intercourse. When he ejaculates, the semen is caught in the end of the sheath. He has to remove his penis carefully from the vagina soon after ejaculating or the sheath may slip off as his penis shrinks back to its normal size.

For extra safety the woman should use a spermicide.* She can either insert cream or jelly into her vagina using a special applicator, or insert a pessary (tablet) with her finger. Pessaries melt inside the vagina.

Both condoms and spermicides are sold at chemists' and drugstores. Condoms are also often sold from slot machines in men's toilets. Besides being a contraceptive, condoms help to prevent the spread of infections, including the one which causes AIDS.

Safe period

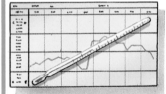

Temperature graph

In theory a woman can only become pregnant during about three days each month. This is the time it takes for an ovum to travel down the uterine tube. Sperm can live inside the woman's body for about two days. This means that if a couple do not have intercourse from about two days before ovulation until about three days after, conception should not take place.

The trouble with this "safe period" method of contraception is that it is extremely difficult to predict ovulation. Couples try to work it out from the dates of the woman's periods; by noting fluctuations in her temperature during her cycles; and by examining a fluid produced by the cervix for changes in its appearance. Even using all three methods, the failure rate is high.

Sterilization

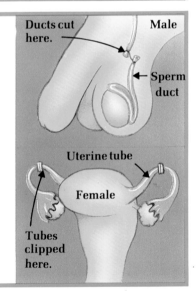

Ducts cut here.

Male

Sperm duct

Uterine tube

Female

Tubes clipped here.

This is a surgical operation to make someone permanently incapable of having children. Generally people only have a sterilization if they already have children and are certain they do not want any more.

Male sterilization is called vasectomy. This is easier to do than female sterilization because the male sex organs are outside the body. Under local anaesthetic, the sperm ducts are cut and tied so that sperm cannot pass down them to the penis. Sterilized men can still ejaculate.

Female sterilization is done under a general anaesthetic. The most usual method is for the uterine tubes to be closed by a clip or plastic ring so that ova cannot pass down them. The woman still has periods. Both men and women can still have a normal sex life.

*Spermicides are not effective used on their own.

Non-methods of contraception

Here are a few of the most common myths about contraception. "The woman cannot become pregnant if . . .

1. . . . the man withdraws his penis from the vagina before he ejaculates." This is untrue because sperm leak out of the penis before ejaculation. If the man ejaculates near the vagina after withdrawal, sperm may still get into it.

2. . . . she lies on top of the man during intercourse or if the couple both stand up." Gravity may mean that fewer sperm swim up into the uterus but very many still will.

3. . . . she is having a period." Sperm can swim through menstrual blood and there may be an ovum in one of the ducts even though it is early in the cycle.

4. . . . she goes to the toilet immediately after intercourse." The sperm will not be flushed out of the body because the vagina and urethra are completely separate.

5. . . . it is the first time she has had intercourse or she has only just started having periods." It is true that some girls start having periods before they are ovulating properly but, as a rule, any woman who has started her periods, or is about to have her first period, may become pregnant.

6. . . . she does not have an orgasm." Contractions of the uterus during orgasm may help to suck the sperm in but they also enter quite easily without them.

Failure rate

You can see how reliable different methods of contraception are below. The figure given shows how many women in a hundred get pregnant using that method for a year.

Combined pill	almost 0%
Mini-pill	2%
IUD	2-4%
Diaphragm and spermicide	3%
Condom and spermicide	3%
Safe period	7-15%
Sterilization	almost 0%
No contraception	80%

The future

At present there is no ideal method of contraception. None is completely effective and without side effects. Research is being done all the time into new methods. These include a morning-after pill; pills or injections of slow-release hormones which would prevent ovulation for several months; a male pill which would prevent sperm production; a special sponge which would work in a similar way to the diaphragm, and a kit for a woman to work out the time of ovulation from the level of certain hormones in her urine.

Abortion

This is not a method of contraception but an operation to end a pregnancy once it has begun. The contents of the woman's uterus are sucked or scraped out, or, if pregnancy is quite advanced, she is given drugs which bring on labour (the birth-process). The risks of the operation include infection.

In many countries abortion is illegal. In others it is legal only under certain conditions. In Britain, for example, it is legal up to the 28th week of pregnancy. Two doctors have to agree that the pregnancy would harm the mother's physical or mental health or that there is a substantial risk of the baby being born handicapped. Anyone under 16 has to have her parents' consent to an abortion.

Food

A healthy diet is important at any age but it is especially necessary at puberty when you are growing and developing very fast. Food, combined with oxygen in the air you breathe, is a fuel which helps you to grow and gives you energy. Different types of food do different jobs in your body so you need to eat a good balance of all the different types. Water, too, is essential.

Protein

Over ten per cent of the human body is made of a substance called protein, so you need to eat protein to grow and for your body to repair itself. For this reason, protein is especially important at puberty. Good sources are lean meat, fish, cheese, eggs, milk, nuts and beans.

Carbohydrates

These provide most of your energy. There are two forms: starches and sugars. It is better to eat starchy foods, such as bread, potatoes, rice and pasta, rather than sweet foods such as cakes, biscuits, chocolate and ice cream or sweetened drinks. Sugar has no benefits apart from giving energy and it is very bad for your teeth.

Fats

These also give you energy. There are two types of fat: "saturated", which is found in animal products such as meat, butter, lard, cream and most margarines and "polyunsaturated", which is found in non-animal products such as liquid vegetable oils, certain margarines and nuts. Experts think that eating too much saturated fat may contribute to heart disease.

Vitamins and minerals

You need small amounts of about 15 different vitamins and 20 minerals for essential chemical processes to take place in your body. The vitamins and minerals are found in a wide range of foods. If you eat a balanced diet, it is not necessary to take vitamin or mineral supplements.

Calcium is an example of a mineral. It is found in foods such as milk and cheese and is important at puberty because it makes your bones and teeth strong. Salt is also an essential mineral though people in developed countries usually eat more of it than is necessary and this may play a part in heart disease.

Fibre

This is not really a food. It consists of a type of carbohydrate that you cannot digest. This travels through your digestive tract in bulk making the muscles of your intestines work efficiently, preventing constipation. Fibre may also help prevent serious diseases of the intestines like cancer. It is found in vegetables, fruit, wholemeal bread and pasta, wholegrain cereals, brown rice, pulses, beans and nuts.

Food groups

Dieticians divide food into the five groups shown here. You need at least two foods from groups 1, 3 and 4 and one from groups 2 and 5 every day.

1. Lean meat, fish, eggs, cheese, lentils, beans and nuts.

2. Bread, potatoes, cereals, rice, pasta (preferably wholegrain varieties).

3. Milk, cheese, yoghurt.

4. Fruit, vegetables.

5. Fats and oils.

Weight

Your weight increases even more spectacularly than your height at puberty as a result of your larger bones and internal organs, and more muscle and fat. The female sex hormones make females gain more fat than males. This is an energy store they can draw on during pregnancy. It is not easy to suggest ideal weights, as people are such different builds.

Age 10
55% of final weight

59% of final weight

Calories

About 40 Calories

About 340 Calories

The amount of energy that can be produced from food is measured in kilojoules or Calories. Different foods have different numbers of Calories. How many calories people need depends on how much energy they use up. Going through puberty takes such a lot of energy that you need as many Calories then as a full-grown adult does. Males generally use more energy than females because they are bigger.

Male at puberty 2,900 Calories a day approx.

Female at puberty 2,150 Calories a day approx.

Being too fat

Any calories which are not converted into energy are stored as fat under your skin. On average, fat people die younger and suffer more from certain illnesses, including heart disease, than thin people. If you think you may be too fat, ask a doctor or a dietician. If you weigh over 13kg (two stone) more than the average weight of all your friends, you may well be eating too many fattening foods. Fats have the most calories, followed by carbohydrates. Try eating less of these foods, especially fried foods such as chips and sugary foods and drinks. Most convenience foods are in this category. Fibre will fill you up without giving you calories. Don't be tempted onto a crash diet. These are unbalanced and you will put back any weight you lose once you stop the diet.

Anorexia nervosa

This serious illness mainly affects girls at puberty. They become obsessed with slimming, thinking they are fat when they are not. An anorexic loses weight dramatically, stops having periods and denies that anything is wrong. The cause may be psychological – perhaps the girl does not want to grow up and tries to keep her childlike shape by starving herself.

Exercise

Exercise is an important part of good health. By making sure you get plenty of exercise during puberty, you help your body to develop as fully as possible. Exercise makes not only the muscles of your skeleton strong but also your heart, which is a muscle too, your lungs and your bones. The younger you are when you start getting fit, the easier you will find it and the more likely you are to avoid certain illnesses, especially heart and circulatory disease, as you get older.

What exercise can do?

Exercise can have many benefits. Here are some of them.

Weight-training

Cycling

Dancing

Keep-fit exercises

Relaxation

1. Exercise makes you strong by increasing the size and strength of your muscles. Without it, muscles waste and turn to fat.

2. It keeps your joints supple so they do not stiffen up and cause aches and pains.

3. It makes you breathe deeper and take in more oxygen. Food you eat must be combined with oxygen inside your body before it can give you energy.

4. It strengthens your heart so that it pumps blood more efficiently. This means it can do more work with less effort. Just running for a bus can strain an unfit person's heart.

5. It improves your circulation by making your blood vessels more elastic and opening up new channels. This means that food and oxygen, which are carried in your blood, get round your body more efficiently.

6. It improves your speed of reaction, co-ordination and grace by making your brain and nervous system work more efficiently.

7. It helps to keep you slim by using up calories.

8. It helps you relax and overcome stress, which can cause illness. You feel generally healthier.

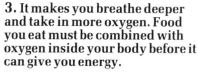

Gymnastics

Running

Tennis

Feeling healthier

What exercise to choose?

Almost any type of exercise is better than none, but for general health and fitness it is best to do a sport which has as many of the benefits shown on the left as possible. These include swimming, football, aerobics, energetic dancing and cycling. Swimming is the best general exercise of all.

Posture

Good posture is quite difficult to learn but it is well worth the effort. Once you know how to stand or sit properly, it is actually less tiring than slumping as it places less strain on your body.

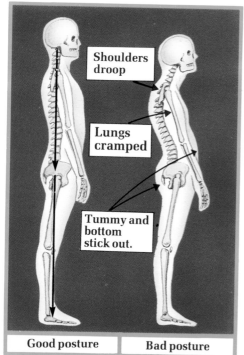

Shoulders droop

Lungs cramped

Tummy and bottom stick out.

| Good posture | Bad posture |

Try to imagine a vertical line running through your pelvis from just behind your ear to just in front of your ankle as shown in the diagram on the left. The one on the right shows the strain put on your body by standing incorrectly.

Sleep

You will probably find you need quite a lot of sleep at puberty because you are growing and using up so much energy. Most 10-14 year-olds need about ten hours sleep a night and 14-18 year-olds about nine but it can vary. The best guide to how much sleep you need is the way you feel.

The reason for sleep is not really understood. During sleep your muscles relax and your heart and breathing rates fall, so it may be a period of recovery and repair for the body. Dreaming may be an important part of learning.

Rest

Rest can be physical relaxation such as sleep or just a change of activity. After exercising hard, sitting and reading a book will rest your muscles and heart. After studying hard, exercise will rest your brain.

Shoes

Your feet are not fully formed until you are about 20, so it is important to wear well-fitting shoes right through puberty. If your shoes are too short, your feet will not grow properly; if they are too narrow or pointed, you may get corns or painful bunions; if they are not flexible your muscles will not develop properly. High heels alter the natural distribution of your weight, causing strain to your feet and to your body as a whole.

Smoking and drinking

Both alcohol and the nicotine in tobacco are drugs and they are addictive. This means that the body gets used to having these substances and can become disturbed without them. It is known that smoking damages your health and can cause serious diseases. For instance, one third of all cases of cancer are thought to be directly related to cigarette smoking. Many people ignore these health hazards and continue to smoke and drink heavily and will try to encourage you to do so. Don't copy them – it is not clever to smoke or drink.

Smoking

1

It is estimated that every cigarette shortens the smoker's life by 14 minutes. Most heavy smokers actually die of diseases caused by smoking. Non-smokers are at risk too just by being in a smoky atmosphere.

It is always worth giving up smoking. Unless disease has already set in, the risks gradually decrease until, ten years after giving up, they almost disappear.

Two of the most poisonous chemicals in tobacco smoke are tar and nicotine.

2

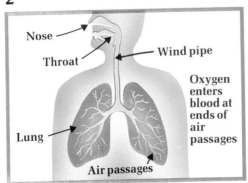

Nose

Throat

Wind pipe

Oxygen enters blood at ends of air passages

Lung

Air passages

The air you breathe has to be cleaned before it reaches the lowest part of your lungs. This is the purpose of the slippery liquid called mucus which you have in your nose and upper air passages. The mucus traps dirt and bacteria, while tiny hairs called cilia waft the mucus away from your lungs towards your nose and throat.

3

The tar in tobacco smoke irritates the air passages, making them narrower, increasing mucus production and making the cilia less efficient so that the mucus, dirt and bacteria stay in the lungs. This causes "smoker's cough", which is really a symptom of bronchitis (inflammation of the air passages) and makes the lungs more prone to infection.

4

Ninety per cent of lung cancer occurs in smokers and tar is thought to be the substance responsible for this.

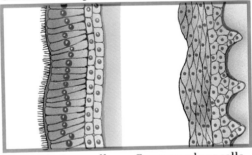

Healthy lung cells.   Cancerous lung cells.

5

Nicotine acts on the brain and nervous system and may be the substance which gives some smokers pleasure. It also makes people unused to smoking feel faint and sick. Nicotine makes the heart beat faster and narrows the blood vessels, contributing to heart and circulatory disease.

Alcohol

Alcohol is a depressant drug, which means that it slows down all the body processes. Small doses make people feel relaxed and confident. Larger doses slow your reactions and affect judgement and co-ordination, which is why it is very dangerous to drink and drive. The drinker may become sick and dizzy, or even fall unconscious, adding the danger of choking on the vomit.

Spirits	Wine	Beer
40% alcohol approx.	12% alcohol approx.	5% alcohol approx.

These effects depend partly on how concentrated the alcohol is in the drink. Spirits, such as whisky or vodka, are the strongest, then wine, then beer. The person's size, and how used they are to alcohol also count. Large people are usually more resistant to alcohol than small ones.

The long term effects of heavy drinking include getting fat, as alcohol contains calories, though no nourishment; inflammation of the stomach leading to ulcers; shrivelling and scarring of the liver (cirrhosis), and damage to the brain, kidneys and muscles, including the heart.

The brain of a person who regularly drinks heavily struggles constantly against the depressant effect of the alcohol to keep them awake. If they then stop drinking, their brain carries on compensating which makes the person excited, nervous, shaky and fidgety until they get another drink. This is an example of dependence.

Illegal drugs

There are a number of drugs which are extremely dangerous and their use and sale is illegal (except under very strict medical supervision). These include heroin and cocaine. They are very highly addictive and you should avoid them completely. Most addicts suffer serious physical or psychological problems. Some die. Do not believe anyone who tells you that a little will do you no harm. This is not true. Don't make the mistake, either, of thinking that heroin is only dangerous if it is injected. Smoking and sniffing it are just as bad. If it is injected using shared equipment, there is an added risk of infection with the AIDS virus (see page 44).

Beware of being offered these drugs by their slang names, which include junk, smack, coke and snow. If you are offered any strange powders or pills, refuse them whatever they are called. You should also refuse any cigarette that is passed around from person to person. It may contain cannabis, another illegal drug (also known as marijuana, pot, grass or hash), or even heroin. You have no way of knowing what is in it.

Sniffing

Inhaling the chemicals in glue, petrol or aerosol sprays has a similar effect on the nervous system to alcohol, but is much more dangerous. There have been many cases of sudden and unexplained death after sniffing. The chemicals can severely damage the brain, liver, kidneys, lungs and bones. Sniffing from a plastic bag can also cause death by suffocation.

Other drugs

Even pills, tablets, powders and other drugs which you can buy from chemists, or drugstores without a prescription, such as aspirins and cold remedies, can damage your health or kill you if you take too many or take them too often. They are all chemicals which are not natural to your body. If you have a headache, ask yourself if you really need an aspirin or if lying down quietly and relaxing might work just as well. You should never take any drug which has been prescribed for someone else.

Keeping clean

Keeping clean becomes more important at puberty than it was during childhood. This is because your skin starts producing more of the substances which can cause unpleasant smells or even ill-health if they are not washed off regularly.

Skin

This picture shows a slice through your skin so you can see what it is like below the surface.

Surface skin: your surface skin is called the epidermis. Its top layer is dead and is constantly being worn away as you come into contact with things. It is then replaced by skin from a layer lower down in the epidermis.

Sebaceous gland: these produce an oily substance called sebum which coats your hair and skin, helping to keep them waterproof and supple. At puberty, the glands start producing more sebum and this can cause greasy hair and spots.

Sweat gland: even when you are not hot, sweat is constantly coming up to the surface of your skin from your sweat glands and coming out through your pores. The sweat rids your body of waste and helps to keep your temperature stable. At puberty, you start to sweat more.

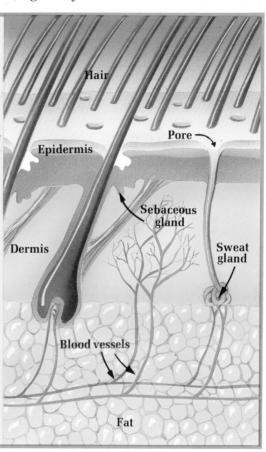

Hair

Epidermis

Pore

Sebaceous gland

Dermis

Sweat gland

Blood vessels

Fat

Washing

You need to wash every day to get rid of dirt, dead skin, sebum and sweat.

Your sweat glands are most numerous under your arms and around your genitals so it is important to wash these parts of your body every day, even if you do not have an all-over shower.

Armpits

Many people find that the numerous sweat glands under their arms make them sweat a lot, especially if they are excited or nervous. Using an underarm deodorant or anti-perspirant helps to stop smells developing before you have a chance to wash. Deodorants work by slowing down the growth of bacteria on the sweat and anti-perspirants make you sweat less by closing some of your pores.

Teeth

Most people have all their adult teeth by about age 16, except for the four wisdom teeth, which come through later. To guard against tooth and gum disease, you should brush your teeth at least twice a day.

Tooth decay is caused by bacteria that feed on sugar in your mouth. They multiply and form a substance called plaque. This contains acids that eat holes into the tooth. If these are not filled, the tooth eventually starts to ache, and an infection or abscess may develop. The tooth may become loose if the gum is damaged.

It is therefore important to go to the dentist regularly. You can help by eating less sugar and by using fluoride toothpaste, which helps strengthen the teeth.

Genitals

Urine, vaginal fluids, menstrual blood, semen and smegma are all quite clean, though once they leave the body bacteria can breed on them as well as on the sweat produced in the area. Bacteria can enter the body through the vagina, urethral opening or penis, so you need to wash the genital area every day.

The rectum contains many bacteria, so it is important, especially for females, to wash and dry from front to back to avoid spreading them to the nearby vagina or urethra. Males need to roll back their foreskin and wash gently underneath.

Wash with mild soap and warm water. Don't use deodorant or anti-perspirant in the genital area, as these can cause irritation or infection. After washing, remember to put on clean underwear.

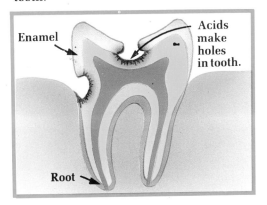

Enamel

Acids make holes in tooth.

Root

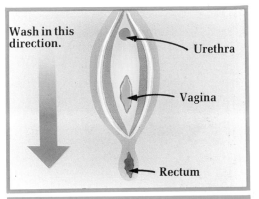

Wash in this direction.

Urethra

Vagina

Rectum

How to clean your teeth

It is important to clean your teeth thoroughly rather than vigorously. Hold the brush at a slight angle and brush up and down, not across, with small strokes, so that the bristles get between your teeth. Work your way right round your mouth and brush the backs of your teeth as well as the fronts. For this it is easiest to hold the brush vertically.

This picture shows the correct way to clean your front teeth.

Discharges

A certain amount of vaginal discharge is normal in females. The vagina's lubricating fluid leaks out and so does the fluid produced by the cervix during the menstrual cycle. They vary from clear to milk in colour and have almost no odour. Some girls have a whitish discharge for a few months before their periods start.

If your normal discharge becomes a lot heavier or thicker, changes colour, or starts to smell, itch or burn, it probably means that bacteria which normally live harmlessly in the vagina have got out of hand and you have an infection. The doctor will be able to treat it with pessaries or antibiotics. Males should go to the doctor if they have any discharge at all from the penis.

Face

Many experts say that soap is bad for the skin on your face because it is a detergent and can dry up sebum too much. On the other hand, people at puberty tend to have an excess of sebum anyway and you may find that the cleansing creams and lotions you can buy give you spots, as well as being expensive. The best thing to do is work out what suits your particular skin.

Spots

It is thought that changes in hormone levels during puberty make your sebaceous glands produce an excess of sebum. Your sebaceous glands are most numerous on your face and back. Testosterone is probably the hormone most involved, so that spots, or acne, are more common in males than females.

If the sebum accumulates at the opening of a sebaceous gland, you get a blackhead. If it builds up below the surface you get a whitehead or a reddish lump. The spot may be infected by bacteria.

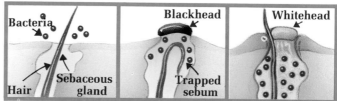

If you are prone to spots, try washing your face frequently using mild, unperfumed or antiseptic soap and warm water. The ultra-violet in sunlight acts as an antiseptic and may help too. Greasy make-up will make spots worse. Cutting out certain foods, such as chips or chocolate, improves some people's spots. Males can try wiping their razor with liquid antiseptic after shaving. If you cannot keep your spots under control, go to the doctor.

You should not really squeeze spots because of the risk of damaging the skin and spreading any infection. If you do squeeze them, make sure your hands are clean and only squeeze blackheads.

Hair

Your hair needs washing to clear it of dirt, dead cells, sebum and sweat. The amount of sebum you produce determines whether you have dry or greasy hair. Greasy hair may need washing as often as once a day; once a week may be enough for dry hair.

Dandruff consists of dead cells from the head. It is more likely to affect those with dry hair. It is rarely infectious and using a "medicated" shampoo is unlikely to help. If it gets very bad, go to the doctor.

Nails

Correct way to cut your big toenail.   Wrong way to cut your big toenail.

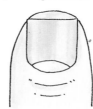 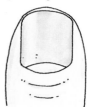

Keep your nails clean by scrubbing underneath with a nail brush.

You can cut your finger nails using scissors or nail clippers, or file them with an emery board. Metal files are not a good idea as they can split the nails. If your nails break easily, keep them short.

For your toenails you need very sharp scissors. Cut the nails straight across. Shaping them can make the edges of the nail grow into the flesh and, if they actually break the skin, cause an infection. This is an ingrowing toenail.

Growing up and your feelings

As you become physically and emotionally more mature, you become more independent and your relationships with the people around you also alter. Some people find these changes quite stressful at times.

It often helps to remember that other people are experiencing the same thing, and that older people probably went through similar experiences at one time. The way you feel may also be affected by physical changes in your body, over which you have no control.

Independence

As you grow up you will probably want to take more responsibility for your own life and actions. This can sometimes cause conflict with your parents, who have to adjust to the idea that you are becoming more independent.

Identity

Thinking about what kind of person you are and about what you want to do and be in the future is an important part of growing up. It can feel lonely and confusing sometimes, coming to terms with your adult personality.

Friends

Most teenagers make close friends and some even fall in love. You may form a close group of friends, which can be fun. Beware of feeling that you must always do what the rest of the group do, especially if you feel uncomfortable or unhappy about it.

Moods

At times you may feel moody and irritable. Changes in your body's hormone levels can be partly to blame for this. Things usually improve as you get used to your adult body and feelings.

Shyness

Many adolescents suffer from shyness. They lack confidence in their looks and personality. How much you suffer and how you cope depends on your individual character. Remember that others often feel shy even if they do not look it.

43

AIDS

What is AIDS?

AIDS stands for acquired immune deficiency syndrome. It is a condition in which a person's immune system, which defends the body against disease, breaks down. This means that the person is likely to get illnesses which they would normally fight off easily. These illnesses can be fatal.

What causes AIDS?

AIDS is caused by a virus called HIV (human immunodeficiency virus). No-one really knows where the virus first came from. A large number of people who have the virus in Western countries are homosexual men but other people can get it too. In Africa, men and women are affected equally. Only some of the people infected with the virus have so far gone on to develop AIDS.

What does the AIDS virus do?

When someone catches any virus, certain of the white blood cells in their body start producing antibodies which attack and kill the virus. The AIDS virus can actually destroy these white blood cells so that the person is unable to fight off infections.

How is the virus passed on?

The virus lives in body fluids such as semen and blood. There are two main ways in which it is passed on from one person to another. One is when semen from an infected person enters another person's body during sexual activity.

The other is when an infected person's blood gets into another person's body. For this reason drug abusers who inject using shared equipment are particularly at risk.

Women who have the virus can pass it on to their baby during pregnancy, at birth or, possibly, in breast milk.

Medical research and AIDS

There is so far no cure for AIDS although a lot is now known about the virus. Doctors can find out whether someone has the virus by testing their blood to see if it contains anti-HIV antibodies. A great deal of research is being done to try to produce more effective drugs for treating people with AIDS and to develop a vaccine so that people could be immunized against it. In the meantime, people are being advised of the ways of reducing their risk of getting the virus.

Preventing the spread of AIDS

The fewer sexual partners a person has, the less risk they have of coming into contact with someone who has the virus. If a person's partner is infected, having vaginal or anal intercourse or oral sex (see the glossary) is risky. Using a condom during intercourse, especially with a spermicide, helps to reduce the risk.

Because of the risk of getting infected blood in the bloodstream, anything which punctures the skin is risky unless it has been properly sterilized. This includes ear-piercing equipment, tattooing and acupuncture needles.

Drug abusers who inject drugs should never share equipment.

It is unwise to share razors or toothbrushes (because many people's gums bleed when they brush their teeth).

Ways in which the AIDS virus is not passed on

The AIDS virus only survives for a short time outside the body so it is not passed on by ordinary everyday contact. You cannot get the virus by touching an infected person or objects used by an infected person such as towels or toilet seats. There is no known case of anyone getting the virus from saliva, for example by kissing or sharing crockery, or from tears, although these are both body fluids. It seems that, although the virus can live in these fluids, it cannot be passed on through them. Swimming pools are also safe because chlorine kills the virus.

In many countries, including Britain, needles and syringes used by doctors, nurses, dentists and other medical staff are always sterilized between patients, a new needle is used for each donor of blood to the blood transfusion service and all blood is tested for AIDS before being given to anyone needing a transfusion.

Glossary

Here are some words you may hear and not know the meanings of. If the word you want is not listed below, try looking in the index at the back of this book, as it may be explained elsewhere.

Acne. The name given to the condition of having lots of spots, usually on the face, upper chest, back and shoulders during puberty. It is a combination of inflamed and pus-containing spots and blackheads, probably caused by hormone activity.

Adultery. Sexual intercourse between a person who is married and someone who is not their husband or wife.

AIDS (Acquired Immune Deficiency Syndrome). See page opposite.

Amenorrhea. Absence of periods.

Anal intercourse. Intercourse in which the penis enters the rectum (back passage).

Aphrodisiac. A substance which increases sexual desire.

Birth control. Contraception.

Blue movie. Pornographic film (see below).

BO. Body odour, caused by not washing often enough.

Brothel. House where prostitutes have sex with their clients.

Calendar method. Unreliable method of contraception which involves predicting a "safe period" for intercourse from the dates of the woman's periods.

Castration. Removal of a male's testes.

Celibacy. Not having sexual intercourse for a longish period of time.

Chastity. Virginity or celibacy (see below).

Child abuse. Mistreating a child, that is anyone under 16, including forcing or persuading her/him into sexual activity. In many countries, including Britain, this is illegal and there are organizations which help children who are being mistreated (see the end of the book).

Clap. Slang word for gonorrhea (see below).

Coitus. Sexual intercourse.

Coitus interruptus. The withdrawal method of contraception (see below).

Copulation. Sexual intercourse.

Crabs. Pubic lice (see below).

Curse, the. Slang word for menstrual period.

Cystitis. Inflammation of the bladder, which causes pain when going to the toilet. Cystitis is usually caused by bacterial infection and is more common in females than males.

Dutch cap. The contraceptive diaphragm.

Erotic. To do with sexual love; producing sexual desire.

Family planning. Contraception; birth control.

Feminist. Someone who wants to improve the rights of women.

Flasher. Someone who displays their genitals in public.

French letter. Slang expression for condom.

Gonorrhea. One of the most common sexually transmitted diseases. It can usually be cured by antibiotics.

Gynaecologist. Doctor who specializes in diseases of the female reproductive system.

Hermaphrodite. Someone who has both male and female sexual features.

Herpes (genital). Also called herpes type 2. A sexually transmitted disease for which no cure is yet known. There is no connection between genital herpes and herpes simplex (also known as herpes type 1) which is a cold sore.

Hysterectomy. Operation to remove a woman's uterus.

Impotence. Inability to get an erection or inability of a male to have an orgasm.

Incest. Sexual intercourse between two people who are too closely related to be legally married, e.g. brother and sister, father and daughter.

IUCD. Intra-uterine contraceptive device. (Same as IUD.)

Libido. Sex drive.

Male chauvinist pig. A sexist male who treats females as though they are inferior to males and should not have the same rights.

Masochist. Someone who gets pleasure from having pain inflicted on them.

Missionary position. The most usual position for sexual intercourse with the couple lying facing each other and the man on top.

Molest. To make unwanted sexual advances to someone.

NSU (Non-specific urethritis). Inflammation of the urethra – the tube leading from the bladder to the outside of the body. This is a sexually transmitted disease which affects males only.

Nymphomaniac. Woman with uncontrollable sexual desire.

Oral sex. Stimulation of the genitals by mouth.

Paedophile. Adult who is sexually attracted to children.

Perversion. Abnormal sexual activity.

Petting. Same as snogging (see below).

Phallus. Image of an erect penis. If something is described as phallic, it resembles an erect penis.

Platonic (friendship). Non-sexual.

Pornography. Pictures or writing aimed at producing sexual arousal.

Pox. Slang word for syphilis (see below).

Premature ejaculation. Male orgasm and ejaculation which are reached too quickly.

Promiscuity. Sexual intercourse with several different casual aquaintances over a short period of time.

Prostitute. Person who has sex with someone in return for payment.

Pubic lice. A sexually transmitted disease caused by a blood-sucker called the crab louse which lives in pubic hair.

Rape. Forcing a woman to have sexual intercourse against her will.

Reproduction. Production of offspring.

Rhythm method. The safe period method of contraception.

Sadist. Someone who gets pleasure from inflicting pain.

Sexist. Someone who thinks people should behave in a particular way because of their sex.

Sexual harassment. Making of unwanted sexual advances to someone; molesting.

Sixty-nine. Simultaneous oral stimulation of the genitals, so-called because of the position of the couple's bodies. Also referred to in French as soixante-neuf.

Snogging. A slang word describing sexual contact which involves kissing and touching the partner's body but does not include intercourse.

Sodomy. Anal intercourse between two males.